HOME SERIES

HOME SERIES
APARTMENTS

BETA-PLUS

CONTENTS

P. 4-5
Olivier Dwek and Caroline Notté
transformed a stable block into
a beautiful loft.
The padded seat in the centre is
a Notté creation, in calf leather
by Vanhamme. Vanhamme also
created the wengé table. The
lamp beside the radiator is an
Ingo Maurer design.

P. 6
This dining room in a city
apartment can be seen from the
kitchen through two tinted
windows. A Flos ceiling light
(model: Taraxacum), a Maxalto
table and Zanotta chairs in calf
leather (model: Lea). A Limited
Edition carpet. Design:
Laurence Sonck.

FOREWORD

T he transformation and interior design of apartments and lofts calls for a special approach.

Apartments are designed for city lifestyles and their specifications may be more restrictive than for houses, often having less available space and a lack of natural light. They also have to offer a refuge from the aggressive world outside, with its noise and pollution. All of these factors combine to make city apartments a real design challenge and an appealing exercise in interior design: improving the circulation between the various living spaces, adapting the layout to modern lifestyles, creating views through the home and making the best possible use of the available space.

Restoring industrial buildings is no simple task. These atypical properties, which often have unusual designs, are popular with fans of unconventional layouts and spaces. The trend for living in lofts and converted industrial properties satisfies a number of modern living requirements: a large amount of space, a flexible layout and the freedom to furnish the property as you wish. This tendency is all about giving a neglected space a new lease of life and the challenge of creating an unusual, very individual home. However, it is a very complex procedure to restore such a property to its former glory, when it was not originally intended as a residential property.

Furnishing compact volumes, decorating a "box" that has no character, integrating different functions to create a harmonious home: this can be a tricky job for the architect and interior designer.

This book presents recent projects by renowned architects and designers who have responded magnificently to these challenges. These classic and contemporary apartments and lofts, some spread over two or even three floors, have all been transformed into distinctive and impressive homes.

P. 8
A view from the hallway into one of the bedrooms in an apartment designed by Marijke Van Nunen. On the floor, wide, untreated oak planks.

P. 10-11
Architect Pascal Van Der Kelen created this apartment, which features a special alcove designed to accommodate the five-metre-long sofa. Front right, Barcelona chair by Mies van der Rohe.

A MODERN ATMOSPHERE

IN A WEEKEND HOME

nterior architect Ann Gryp completely redesigned the layout of this apartment, which previously consisted of a series of small rooms, to correspond to her client's lifestyle.

The materials and layout of the space were selected in close collaboration with the owners. The result is a simply designed interior, which is easy and pleasant to live in, with sober and natural materials: a tinted wooden floor for all of the living areas, off-white painted walls throughout, double curtains in linen. This is an almost masculine atmosphere, accentuated by the clean lines of the furniture in dark wood.

A view of the living room with an integrated kitchen, as seen from the parents' bedroom through a wide sliding door. The slope of the roof meant the design had to compensate by creating a sense of space. This is also what prompted the interior architect to combine the rooms into a single whole.

Table and chairs from the Maxalto collection. The low surface runs the entire length of the room and serves as a bench where the children can sit to have their breakfast and other meals.

P. 16-17
Flexform chairs. Above the
fireplace, a flat screen
integrated into the wall.

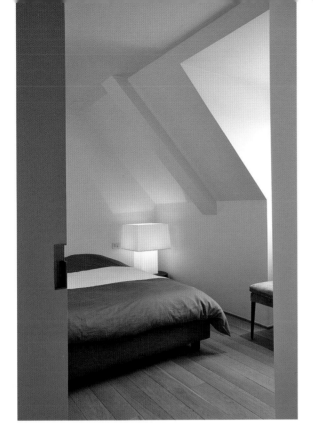

The same desire for simplicity in the parents' bedroom, as seen from the living room.

This room, with its dormitory feel, provides space for six children. It has a symmetrical layout, with a play area, shelves and computer desk in the centre.

The parents' bathroom is a sober, functional space. Here too, the simplicity of materials has been respected.

The walls of the large shower in the parents' bathroom are in square marble mosaic.

AN ECLECTIC LOFT

IN A FORMER GRAIN WAREHOUSE

A rchitect Stéphane Boens transformed this grain warehouse from the mid-twentieth century into a contemporary loft in which antiques and designer pieces are combined in an eclectic fashion.

The spacious, open volume, in which the original pillar structure has been retained, was redesigned to create a huge residential loft (500m^2) over three floors.

In contrast with other lofts, the industrial atmosphere has not been fully exploited here, in order to create an atmosphere of warmth, particularly through the frequent use of solid wood and comfortable, rustic-inspired pieces of furniture.

A look that is a cross between a house and a loft: the structure is a reminder of the building's history, but the materials make this design stand out from typical loft projects.

The same floor throughout the 500m^2 loft: reclaimed pine cheese planks.

All of the armchairs and the desk are
from antiques dealer Axel Vervoordt.
The panels are in aged oak.

The original pillar structure remains
visible throughout this spacious loft.

The minimalist kitchen is a design by John Pawson for Obumex.

A mix of transparency and intimacy in this bedroom and bathroom.
The floor and walls of the bathroom are in mosaic tiles.

THE SUBTLE RENOVATION

OF A PIED-À-TERRE

T his spacious apartment (ca. 180m^2) is situated in a building from the 1970s.

The young architect Olivier Dwek has given the property a fresh, new look.

He retained the original layout of the apartment, but completely renovated the interior, using exclusive, top-quality materials to create a discreet, elegant and cosy atmosphere.

The natural colour palette and the well-proportioned furniture ensure a sophisticated look.

P. 28-31

The seating in the living room is by Donghia: a three-seater Serpentine Club sofa, a Serpentine Club chair and a Serpentine ottoman, all upholstered in silk.

The coffee table is made of ivory piano keys (a creation by Ado Chale). The ivory door handles were created especially for this project. The lamp and the rounded Zig Zag table by Donghia are in maple.

The built-in spotlights in the alcoves are by Kreon. The radiator grilles are in brushed stainless steel. A rare American nut wood for the parquet and a carpet by Oliver Treutlein in pure new wool. Paints by Farrow & Ball.

A silkscreen print by the German artist Penck above the pewter table. Serpentine side chair in leather and maple (with black-cherry finish).

A System 25 Bulthaup kitchen in stainless steel and grey MDF.

Three pieces of Nigerian money from the nineteenth century and a silkscreen print by the Venezuelan artist Soto.

CLASSIC INSPIRATION

IN A SEASIDE APARTMENT

A married couple with adult children decided to leave the city and move to a new apartment on the Belgian coast.

Interior architect Annick Colle designed this large space (around 185m²), situated beside the sea. The period furniture, combined with the pale shades, is indicative of the subtle, calming decor.

Annick Colle selected an under-floor heating system and spotlights because of the low ceilings in the apartment. The halogen spots are by Modular. The oak floor has a bleached finish. Louis XVI armchairs by Michel Ceuterick and a console from the same period by antiques dealer Mestdagh. The mirror is also from Mestdagh. In the background, silk curtains by Rubelli.

Right in the photo, the door to the lift, which goes straight to the hallway of the apartment. Left, the emergency exit, which opens onto the service staircase.
A mirror by Kristine Wyffels above the console (from antiques dealer Mestdagh).

The old washbasin, from Dominique Desimpel, is in white Carrara marble and is harmoniously integrated between the panelled walls.

An Obumex kitchen in painted MDF.
A sliding door, integrated into the low ceiling, separates this space from the other rooms.

The bathroom is also by Obumex and built to a design by Annick Colle. The floor and the stone surfaces are in Civec marble. Madison taps by Dornbracht, in a brass finish.

In the bedroom, a traditionally manufactured Vi-Spring bed. Silk curtains by Rubelli.

A MULTI-FUNCTIONAL DESIGN

T he challenge in this project was to design a weekend home for a family consisting of three generations.

Interior architect Annick Colle designed the plans for a complete transformation of this apartment, including the structural work. Not a single interior wall was spared: all of the small rooms were combined to create an open and cosy design.

The use of ceiling-height doors and sliding panels disguises the limited height of the rooms and also perfectly divides up the available space, creating different atmospheres: from reception rooms to the cosy sitting room. The look is contemporary, with a number of striking twentieth-century designer pieces.

Two built-in sliding panels separate the kitchen from the dining room. Kitchen work surface in Marlin granite with a smoothed finish. To make optimal use of the space, Annick Colle chose classic radiators and built-in spotlights. The table and chairs are by Knoll; the sofa in the foreground is by Christian Liaigre. A carpet by Limited Edition.

The MDF wall panels have a black finish.
Left, two chairs by Christian Liaigre; central in the background, a chaise longue by Herman Miller. Curtains by Souveraine.

Shutters separate the shower room and the bedroom. Optimal use has been made of every room in this 150m^2 apartment. The oak parquet and shutters have a black finish.

The washbasin unit is in MDF with a black finish and a Civec marble surface. Tara taps by Dornbracht. Chestnut mosaic tiles.

The bathroom walls are painted white. This apartment has a serene atmosphere, with no unnecessary frills.

A view of the bathroom from the parents' bedroom.

LIVING BY THE WATER

D utch interior architect Alexandra Siebelink was responsible for designing and furnishing this spacious lakeside apartment.

She created a successful mixture of old, classic elements with a number of contemporary touches, in a natural palette and materials: sand, white, plain materials, such as wood and linen. This is a calm and timeless look.

Right in the photo, a Swedish corner cupboard from the eighteenth century. Extreme left, on the round table, some pieces from the Chinese Han dynasty.

The pale-blue cupboard is from Reims cathedral and dates from the fifteenth century. Some Han pieces in this room too.

P. 46-47
The concrete-look floor also has a contemporary cachet. Front left, a lamp made from an old Burmese water pitcher. Right, Gerrit Rietveld's famous Zig Zag chair. At the back, a dining table in solid oak and comfortable chairs. Right in the background, the table-height gas fire.

An eighteenth-century Swedish table serves as a desk. At the front, an "os de mouton" chair. A Tizio desk lamp by Artemide.

On the piano, a beautiful collection of Han vases. The monochrome work in the background is by Thomas Pihl.

A large teak table with modern chairs. In the background, a summer sitting room.

CREATING

A LUXURIOUS PENTHOUSE

C y Peys & Partners architectural studio coordinated the design and furnishing of this top-floor apartment, transforming it into a luxurious penthouse.

This penthouse resembles a lounge in a luxury designer hotel: attractive, simple, calm. The use of dark varieties of wood and furniture with clean lines give a structure to this beautifully designed space.

Indirect lighting in this dark-tinted fitted unit. A custom-built coffee table, with a gloss finish. A lamp by Christian Liaigre.

Gyproc and sheet steel have given a new look to the existing fireplace. The wooden blinds create a subtle light in the apartment. A chaise longue by B&B Italia and a goatskin carpet with traditional stitching.

P. 52-53
The custom-made bench and indirect lighting create a beautiful atmosphere in the breakfast space.

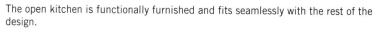
The open kitchen is functionally furnished and fits seamlessly with the rest of the design.

The existing radiators were concealed behind oak planks and covered with dark-tinted wooden grilles. Art by Bruno Vekemans.

The bedroom with concealed access to
the dressing room. The lamp is by
Stéphane Davidts. A satin throw by
Isola.

The mirror and the glass walls of the steam shower were
made specially for this project. Taps, showerhead and a
square washbasin unit from Waterl'Eau.

A lounge atmosphere in the
upstairs corridor: subdued,
indirect lighting in a variety of
colours.

A COSY FAMILY ATMOSPHERE

T wo flats, situated on the Belgian coast, have been joined together to create one spacious apartment where three generations of one family can enjoy their holidays.

The new home has an open and transparent look, but sufficient privacy has still been provided for all of the members of the family.

This project by interior designer Winy Van Aggelpoel was created in close collaboration with Sphere (furniture and soft furnishings) and Sphere Concepts (custom-built work).

The kitchen and the bathrooms were made by Vossaert to a design by Winy Van Aggelpoel.

Simplicity throughout, with soft and natural touches: cotton, linen, wood. The use of subtle shades and the harmony of greys creates a very calming atmosphere.

The curtains and blinds are in crushed linen by De Le Cuona.
Two Henry Dean lanterns on the coffee table (model: Toos, designed by Piet Boon).
The paint was selected from the Paint & Paper Library, which is distributed by Sphere.

Piet Boon designed the sofa (model: Koen) and standing lamps (model: Klaar).

The wooden floor (solid oak parquet with under-flooring) has expansion joints.

P. 58-59
Dining table in solid oak. Cruz chairs by
Meridiani. Wrought-iron doors separate
the kitchen and dining room.

P. 60-61
The custom-built chairs are upholstered with a linen stone material by De Le
Cuona. Amber armchair. The painting is by Laurent Reypens.

P. 62-63
The oak desk is a design by Sphere Concepts.

CONTEMPORARY DESIGN

AND ANTIQUES
IN A TRIPLEX APARTMENT

A real metamorphosis in the stairway. The original stairs were demolished and a metal construction was installed: transparent and easy to maintain. On the left, part of an artwork by Baillieux.

A rchitect Boud Rombouts transformed this historic property (1910), belonging to antiques dealer Opdenakker, to create a spacious triplex apartment of 400m².

In this private apartment, the antiques dealer shows his eclectic vision of interior architecture: antiques and contemporary design combine in a fascinating way, melting together to form a surprising symbiosis.

Light, transparency, space and comfort are the principles behind this home-design concept: the classic layout of the elegant townhouse is literally opened up, with a structure that is reduced to its essence.

The small proportions of the TV and reading room underline the cosiness of these rooms.

Ceiling-height doors throughout (4.5m), a dramatic statement that accentuates the continuity and openness of this space. On the pedestal, a bronze statue of Louis XIV.

Cab chairs by Cassina around a glass table designed by Cozza Mascheroni. The bronze wall lamps are from Paris.

An eastern atmosphere in the guestroom.

Two columns from Argenteuil on an
English commode (17th century).
The floors throughout the property
are in black slate.

A gloss finish for the kitchen. Work surfaces in black granite.

Black mirrors in the kitchen.
In the background, white
blinds filter the daylight.

A cosy atmosphere in the bedroom. An eighteenth-century Italian commode, Napoleon III wall lamps, a Biedermeier bedside table, an antique kilim and modern stools.

The dressing room is also four metres high and has three layers of rails on the left.

PEACE AND QUIET

IN A DUPLEX APARTMENT

C y Peys & Partners interior-design studio transformed part of this rooftop apartment to create a luxurious duplex "pied-à-terre".

The sober decoration is combined with warm earthy shades, high-quality materials and timeless, distinctive furniture. This is not fashionable minimalism, but a top-class apartment with a wonderfully serene atmosphere.

Chairs by Christian Liaigre around a custom-made table in tinted oak. Art by Eric de Smet. Blinds in dark-red linen.

The entire ground floor of this duplex apartment is in tinted oak parquet. Use of the same flooring throughout has created a sense of space. The striped carpet is from Emente.

P. 74-75
A library on the upper floor above the fireplace (on the right) breaks up this large open space.

The office. Custom-built oak cupboards with a pale finish function as a bar. The two padded seats in the foreground are upholstered in a bright orange fabric.

The floor on the ground level is in a luxurious carpet in linen and silk: a cosy, sophisticated atmosphere for these private rooms. Custom-made walls in a pale finish.

The main bathroom is in pale-beige stone with fitted units in light oak.

The main bedroom has a sober, meditative atmosphere. On the bed, a throw by Emente. The oak walls have a pale finish here too.

A DUPLEX APARTMENT

IN A DEAUVILLE-STYLE BUILDING

T his duplex apartment is situated at the top of a seaside apartment in Deauville style.

The first floor contains the entrance hall, toilets, kitchen, dining room and a separate zone including the stairway, a sitting area with two armchairs and a round table, the living room, two bedrooms and a dressing room.

The second floor has an office, a guestroom and a washroom.

Neoo selon Neoo designed the first floor, while Ann Gryp took care of the second floor.

A sitting room beside the window was created between the living room and the dining room. The wooden blinds filter the light in the apartment, without interrupting the view of the seaside town. Left, a large sliding door, designed as panelling, separates this space from the living room.

Storage space beneath the stairs. Most of the rooms (except the kitchen and the bathrooms) have oak parquet flooring.

P. 80-81
A flat screen (above the fireplace), a walk-in bar and a door to the emergency staircase have been built into the panelling in this room.

A built-in cupboard that follows the contours of the roof. The glass door on the right leads into the hallway. To emphasise the verticality, the doors are almost ceiling-height.

P. 82
The kitchen floor, the surfaces and the sink are in the same grey-brown stone. Painted units in solid wood.

Small cupboards to the left and right of the bath. Shower door in enamelled glass.

This bathroom is in red zelliges.

Ann Gryp designed the rooms upstairs.
The panelling in the main bedroom (top photo) is in a taupe paint.
Left, a concealed door to the dressing room.

THE SUBTLE RENOVATION

OF A CONTEMPORARY APARTMENT

nterior designer Sophie Campion's task in this apartment created by Marc Corbiau was to introduce a sober, timeless atmosphere, incorporating some of the owners' favourite pieces of furniture.

This interior is one of Sophie Campion's last projects.

The look is very elegant, yet cosy. An ethnic chic style, accentuated by a number of well-chosen pieces from different places and eras.

A sliding door separates the office from the sitting room. The desk is in bleached oak. A sculpture by Takis.

A Chinese bed serves as a coffee table. An oil painting by Pierre Alechinsky. Two seventeenth-century Spanish jars. The vases are from South Africa.

P. 90-91
The Minotti sofas are in a fabric by Sahco Hesslein. Right in the foreground, a silk Chinese rug. Above the fireplace, a work by Hans Hartung. Between the two sliding doors in the background, a work by Karel Appel. On the table, a Burmese torso.

Curtains and bedspread in linen. To the left of the artwork by the Mexican artist De La Rose, a lamp by Christian Liaigre.

Small, custom-made desk in bleached oak. Right, a Chinese rug. Centre, a work by Alexander Schmitt.

Chairs by InStore and a wrought-iron table. A plate by Christiane Perrochon. Floor in bluestone. Art by Alexander Schmitt.

SANDY SHADES

IN A SEASIDE APARTMENT

nterior architect Philip Simoen transformed a sea-view apartment into a cosy home full of calming, monochrome shades: sand, greige and earthy colours.

The warmth of this interior is reinforced by the choice of sophisticated materials: furniture from Promemoria, Hurel and Flexform, fabrics from Malabar and Canovas, fitted units in aged oak and a teakwood floor.

P. 94-97

The sense of harmony is accentuated by the teakwood floor and the discreet colours. Caffé table and chairs by Promemoria in dark-tinted oak.

Kamla curtains from the Malabar collection, made by Inndekor. An Arfa sofa and armchairs by Philippe Hurel and a bamboo coffee table. Philip Simoen designed the oak wall unit. Lamps by Stéphane Davidts. An oak kitchen unit with a Buxy stone surface.

The floor, sink and bath are in Buxy stone. Walls in sand-coloured Sicis glass mosaic. Tara taps by Dornbracht.

The library, beside the dressing room. A Flexform sofa and a Promemoria table with a leather surface. Lamp by Stéphane Davidts. Fitted oak units.

Philip Simoen designed the fitted oak wardrobes in this bedroom. Quilt and curtains in Veloutine Saint-Germain by Canovas. Wall lights by Christian Liaigre.

IMMACULATE WHITE

FOR A DRAMATIC LOOK

Stefanie Everaert and Caroline Lateur (Doorzon) created the interior of this apartment with a wonderful sea view.

Tom Sileghem, senior interior architect at Obumex, coordinated the technical aspects and the painting.

Van den Weghe did all of the work in natural stone.

The floor of the entire apartment is in Bianco Statuario marble.

The Bianco Statuario creates a beautifully bright atmosphere throughout this home, from the front to the back.

Handmade ceramic tiles from Makkum in the toilet.

Van den Weghe used bars of Emperador Dark marble in the shower.

A CLASSIC AND ECLECTIC STYLE

M arie-Rêve Decoration and interior architect Marc Biermann transformed the second and third floors of an old house to create a private apartment.

This interior is a perfect showcase for the owner's eclectic taste: a meticulous and coherent look, pervaded by the spirit of the eighteenth century and complemented by some contemporary touches and occasional references to the 1940s.

A collection of terracotta Chinese vases on a linen tablecloth. The chairs are also upholstered in linen. Above the table, a crystal chandelier. In the background, to the right of the silk blind, a lamp from antiques dealer Michel Lambrecht.

A varied look in this sitting room on the third floor. Two red armchairs from the 1940s, a coffee table in oak and wrought iron, a Buddha head from Thailand beside a contemporary work by Jean-Marc Louis. A silk blind and a wrought-iron lamp from Michel Lambrecht.

The washbasin and bathtub have oak surrounds with a matte varnish finish. A wool carpet and a stool from China.

Headboard and curtains in grey flannel. A copper chandelier from the 1950s. A Louis XV-style "cabriolet" and a Milleraies carpet. The banquette on the left in the photograph is upholstered in a chestnut-coloured, satin-finish cotton fabric.

CLEAN LINES AND LUXURY

IN AN EXCLUSIVE PENTHOUSE IN LONDON

CarterTyberghein were commissioned to design the interior of the top-floor apartment on the eighteenth floor of a building in the Docklands, with a beautiful view of the Thames.

They used the natural advantages of the apartment as the basis for a design for a luxurious penthouse with a large entrance hall that opens out onto a terrace.

The contrast between dark wood and pale finishes is a theme running throughout the apartment.

Sophisticated fabrics and textures were selected to perfect the cosy look of this home.

A cabinet designed by CarterTyberghein with mirror and wall lights by Van der Straeten. Chairs from Armani Casa on either side of the cabinet. Artworks sourced by CarterTyberghein.

The lift lobby with dark oak walls.

Curved entrance hall leading through to the living room with Accero limestone floor.

Above
The 180° glazed living room with views across the Docklands. Silk and wool rug from Veedon Fleece.

Right
A contemporary fireplace with a Portoro marble surround. A plasma screen is concealed behind panels above the fireplace. To the left and right, double doors leading to the entrance hall and study.

Ceiling-height doors lead through to the living room. Dining chairs upholstered in bronze leather. Custom-made mirrors and Christian Liaigre armchairs.

Kitchen in dark Indian palisander with work surfaces and splashbacks in black glass. Floor in Ebano marble.

Right
Behind the pillar, a drinks cabinet designed for the client. Electrically operated curtains in fabric from De le Cuona run the length of the room.

P. 116
Shelving in dark palisander wood from India behind a desk from JNL.

The guest bedroom with a craquelé finish and bronze handles for the wardrobe doors. Cupboard designed for the client.

Silk and wool mixed carpet flows through the master bedroom suite, adding a cosy touch.

Silk panelling behind the bed gives a luxurious, haute couture look to the bedroom.

The walls in the main bathroom are in Statuario marble. The mirror conceals a TV screen and the vanity unit is finished in metal leaf with a Thassos marble surface.

THE CONTEMPORARY RENOVATION

OF AN OLD APARTMENT

E sther Gutmer's M.E.G. interior-design studio renovated this apartment in a building that dates back to around 1900.

The apartment was initially made up of smaller rooms, so Esther Gutmer started by redesigning the layout.

This interior is streamlined and contemporary with no period details, such as moulding or panelling, to reveal the building's past.

The apartment has a very open and airy feeling throughout, primarily because of the ceiling-height sliding doors.

The use of wooden furniture tempers the apparent severity of this design.

Two sliding doors open into the kitchen, with its chalk-white walls. A Pierre de Vinalmont stone on the floor. Work surface in pearl-coloured Corian. Blinds in pale-grey voile.

In the foreground, a table with a surface in steel and glass (design: Esther Gutmer). An old music score from Galerie Y. David, a Barcelona daybed in chestnut-coloured fabric and a felt carpet. Esther Gutmer selected the wengé table in the dining room (by Christian Liaigre). An oak floor with an aged finish. Sofa in chestnut-coloured linen.

The wall behind the bed is painted in a dark chestnut shade. Shelves in afrormosia wood, tinted in khaki. Two bedside tables designed by Esther Gutmer and created by 3ème Bureau. Two vintage photographs of New York.

A concealed sliding door in afrormosia leads to the dressing room, which is in the same wood.

The washbasin unit is in wengé, chrome and slate (design: Esther Gutmer).
The floor is in large slabs of smooth slate. Taps by Dornbracht in matte nickel.
Two medicine cabinets behind the mirrors. Epoxy wall lights by Liaigre.

The bath has a stone surround.
Linen blinds by De le Cuona.

HOME SERIES

Volume 6 : APARTMENTS

The reports in this book are selected from the Beta-Plus collection of home-design books: www.betaplus.com
They have been compiled in a special series by Le Figaro in French language: Ma Déco

Copyright © 2009 Beta-Plus Publishing / Le Figaro
Originally published in French language

PUBLISHER
Beta-Plus Publishing
Termuninck 3
B – 7850 Enghien
Belgium
www.betaplus.com
info@betaplus.com

PHOTOGRAPHY
Jo Pauwels

DESIGN
Polydem - Nathalie Binart

TRANSLATIONS
Laura Watkinson

ISBN: 9789089440372

P. 126-127
A project by Olivier Dwek and Caroline Notté.